WHERE IN THE WORLD WAS MATT?

Donald Gorbach

ISBN-10 1981509968
ISBN-13 978-1981509966

"WHEN PEOPLE START TO WRITE ARTICLES
ABOUT WHAT MAY BE WRONG WITH THE TODAY SHOW,
YOU KNOW WHERE YOU SHOULD POINT THE FINGER…
POINT IT AT ME…"

— MATT LAUER (WHO KNEW!)

REALITYCOVERBOOKS.COM

www.ingramcontent.com/pod-product-compliance
Lightning Source LLC
Chambersburg PA
CBHW050912260726
48660CB00001B/156